Real Science-4-Kids

Level I

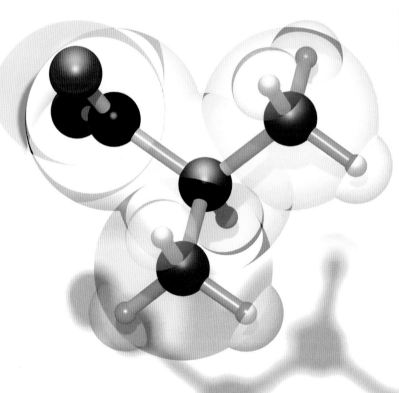

Dr. R. W. Keller

RealScience
4
Kids

Cover design: David Keller
Opening page: David Keller
Illustrations: Rebecca Keller

Copyright © 2004, 2005 Gravitas Publications, Inc.

Real Science-4-Kids: Chemistry Level I-Textbook

ISBN # 0-9749149-0-8

Published by Gravitas Publications, Inc.
P.O. Box 4790
Albuquerque, NM
87196-4790
www.gravitaspublications.com

Printed in Hong Kong

Illustrations
Chapter 9: 9.1 Art Today. Chapter 10: All molecular coordinates were provided by the Brookhaven Protein Data Bank.

Front cover: water molecule showing both bonding of two hydrogens to one oxygen and the van der Waals radii of the atoms

Back cover, inside title page: L-Alanine molecule, one of the amino acids

...knowledge that matters

The Periodic Table of Elements

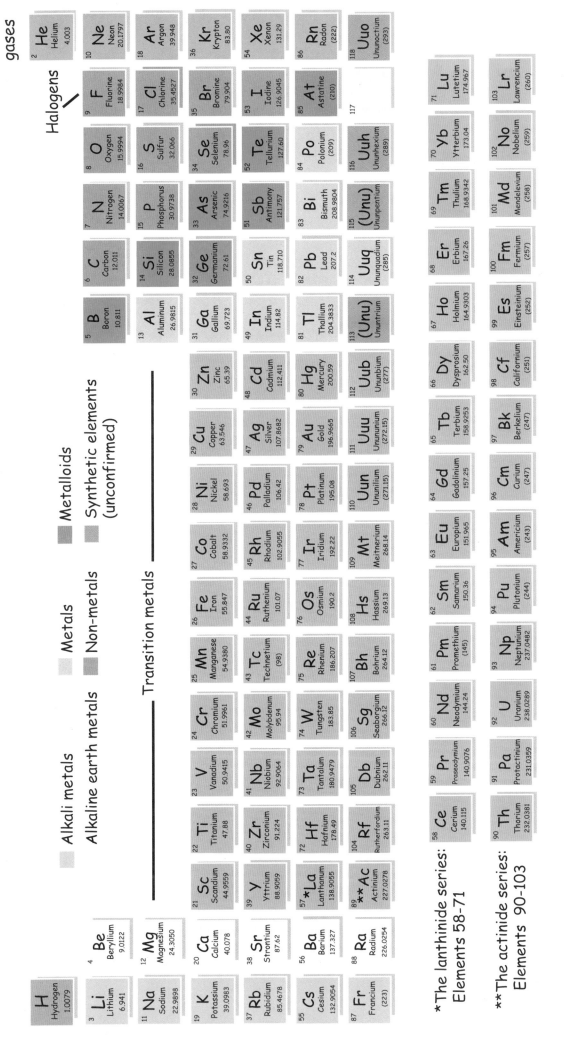

Noble gases

Halogens

Transition metals

Alkali metals

Alkaline earth metals

Metalloids

Metals

Non-metals

Synthetic elements (unconfirmed)

*The lanthinide series:
Elements 58-71

**The actinide series:
Elements 90-103

Chapter 1: Matter

1

H

Hydrogen

1.0079

92

U

Uranium

238.0289

1.1 Introduction

What is chemistry? Have you ever wondered what the world and the objects in the world are made of? What is water exactly? Why do ice cubes float? What are our hair and skin made of? Why is a marble hard but a jellyfish soft?

All of these questions, and others like them, begin the inquiry into that branch of science called chemistry.

Chemistry is the study of matter, which is a general term for what forms all living and nonliving things.

Chemistry is concerned mainly with the properties of matter. All of the items we encounter on a daily basis are made of matter.

Balloons are made of matter.

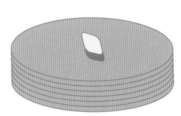

Pancakes are made of matter.

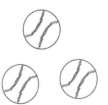

Baseballs are made of matter. Even our bodies are made of matter. But what makes up matter?

1.2 Atoms

The fundamental building blocks of matter are atoms (a'-təms). The word atom comes from the Greek word *atomos*, which means "uncuttable." During the 5th century b.c.. the Greek philosophers proposed the idea that there must be some smallest uncuttable units of matter. They called these units atoms.

Today we know that atoms are composed of even smaller particles called protons (prō'-täns), neutrons (nü'-träns), and electrons (ē'-lek'-träns).

Proton

Protons and neutrons are roughly equal in size, but electrons are very much smaller than both protons and neutrons. Protons, neutrons, and electrons are all much smaller than an atom.

Neutron

Protons and neutrons combine to form the central core or nucleus (nü'-klē-əs) of the atom. The electrons occupy the space surrounding the nucleus. This space is sometimes called the electron cloud.

• Electron

The number of electrons in an atom always equals the number of protons. Notice that, for the helium (hē'-lē-um) atom, there are two protons and two electrons. Sometimes the number of protons also equals the number of neutrons as with helium, but this is not always true.

Helium Atom

neutrons

protons

electrons

Most of the space of an atom is actually filled up by the electron cloud. The central core of an atom takes up only a very small part of the total space.

On the other hand, almost all of the mass of the atom is in the protons and neutrons in the nucleus. The electrons weigh almost nothing compared to the nucleus, yet they take up all the space!

1.3 Periodic table

All of the atoms that make up the world are known. They are called chemical elements or just elements (e´-lǝ-mǝnt). Early in the 19th century, a total of 55 chemical elements were known and many more were being discovered. Their properties were very different from each other and it was difficult to organize them. In 1867, Dmitri Mendeleev (men-dǝ-lē´-ǝv) organized the elements into what is now called the periodic table of elements.

In today's periodic table, the elements are arranged horizontally from left to right in order of increasing atomic number. The atomic number is the number of protons in the nucleus of each atom. For example, carbon has an atomic number of 6, which means it has 6 protons in its nucleus. Oxygen has an atomic number of 8, which means it has 8 protons in its nucleus.

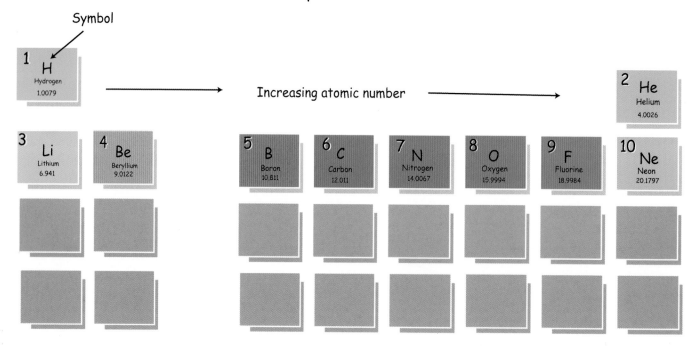

All of the elements have a symbol. For example, hydrogen has the symbol "H" and carbon has the symbol "C." Notice that the symbol is the same as the first letter of the name. This is true for many elements because they have English names, like "O" for oxygen. But some names come from other languages. The name for sodium (sō´-dē-ǝm) comes from the Latin word *natrium* so it has the symbol "Na." Tungsten comes from the German word *wolfram*, so it has the symbol "W." Other examples include gold, which has the symbol "Au" from the Latin word *aurum*, and lead, which has the symbol "Pb" from the Latin word *plumbum*.

As we just saw, the atomic number tells how many protons the atom contains. In an atom, the number of protons equals the number of electrons, so this number is also the number of electrons in an atom. For example, the smallest element is hydrogen (hī'-drō-jen). It has an atomic number of 1, which means it has only one proton. It also has only one electron, since *the number of protons equals the number of electrons.*

Atomic number

1

H

Hydrogen

1.0079

Symbol

Name

Atomic weight

Hydrogen has only one proton and no neutrons.

Though atoms are very small, each one has a weight, called the atomic weight. For most atoms the atomic weight is very close to the sum of the protons and neutrons in the nucleus. Both protons and neutrons have an atomic weight of 1. Electrons are so small that they are given almost no weight at all. The number of neutrons for an atom can be calculated by subtracting the number of protons from the atomic weight.

Atomic number

92

U

Uranium

238.0289

Symbol

Name

Atomic weight

Uranium has 92 protons and 146 neutrons

For example, the atomic weight for hydrogen is 1.0079, which is the number found below the name. To find the number of neutrons, the number of protons (1) is subtracted from the atomic weight (1.0079 or 1); 1 - 1 = 0. This means that hydrogen has no neutrons and only one proton in its nucleus.

The largest naturally occurring element is uranium (yü-rā'-nē-əm). It has an atomic number of 92, which means it has 92 protons and 92 electrons. It has an atomic weight of 238.0289. To calculate the number of neutrons, the number of protons is subtracted from the atomic weight (238 - 92 = 146), so uranium has 146 neutrons.

Vertically, the elements are arranged according to their chemical properties. All of the elements in a single column undergo similar chemical reactions and have similar chemical properties. All of the elements on the far right-hand column of the periodic table are called the noble gases. They are similar to each other because they don't react with other atoms or molecules. The elements on the far left-hand column are called the alkali (al'-kə-lī) metals. They are similar to each other because they react with lots of different atoms or molecules.

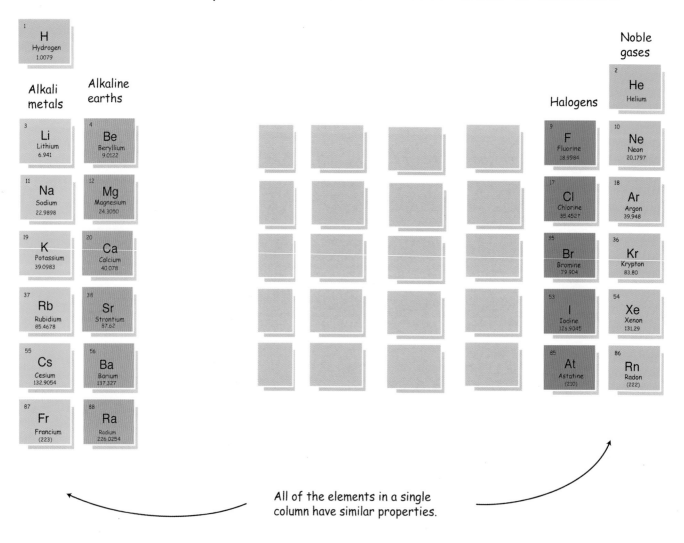

All of the elements in a single column have similar properties.

The periodic table of elements organizes a lot of information about the elements and their chemical properties. This table helps chemists predict the behavior of the elements and how they might interact with each other. Before all of the naturally occurring elements were known, Mendeleev was able to predict many of the properties of the missing elements using the organization of his table. The success of his predictions and the organization of his chart led to its overall acceptance as a major scientific accomplishment.

1.4 Summary

Here are the most important points to remember from this chapter:

○ All things, both living and nonliving, are made of atoms.

○ Atoms are made of protons, neutrons, and electrons.

○ In an atom, *the number of protons equals the number of electrons.*

○ All atoms (or elements) are found in the periodic table of elements.

○ The elements are arranged on the periodic table in groups that are similar.

Chapter 2 : Molecules

2.1 From atoms to molecules

As we saw earlier, everything is made of atoms. Sometimes things are made of a single type of atom, like gold or silver, and sometimes things are made of more than one type of atom, like salt, which is a combination of sodium and chlorine. When two or more atoms combine with each other, they make a molecule.

Recall that atoms are made of protons, neutrons, and electrons. Protons and neutrons are located in the center of an atom while the electrons surround them. When two atoms come together, sometimes they will "stick" to each other. When this happens, a molecule is formed.

2.2 Forming bonds

How do atoms stick to each other to make molecules? As it turns out, *electrons* make atoms "stick" to each other. They do this by sharing the space inside their electron clouds.

For example, a single hydrogen atom has just one electron. When another hydrogen atom gets close enough, the two electron clouds combine, and the electrons from each of the two atoms share the combined space.

When this happens, the two atoms are said to form a bond. This simply means that the two atoms are now connected, or "stuck," to each other.

Two separate hydrogen atoms

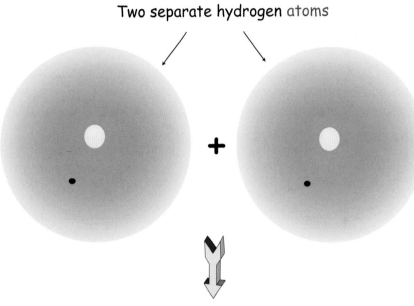

One single hydrogen molecule

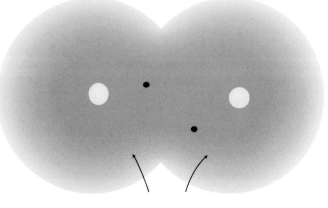

Space shared by both electrons

2.3 Types of bonds

There are two different kinds of bonds and they differ only in how they share their electrons. Sometimes electrons are shared between the two atoms. This kind of bond can be called a shared electron bond. Sometimes one atom takes more electrons for itself. This kind of bond can be called an *unshared electron* bond. Molecules that have shared electron bonds behave very differently from molecules that have unshared electron bonds. This difference is quite important because it determines the way molecules interact with other molecules.

2.4 Shared electron bonds

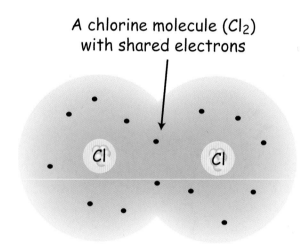

A chlorine molecule (Cl_2) with shared electrons

The hydrogen molecule that we just saw is an example of a bond where the electrons are *equally* shared. Because the atoms are identical (they are both hydrogens), one atom cannot take more electrons for itself than the other atom. This results in a bond with *shared* electrons and in this particular case the electrons are equally shared. A bond with shared electrons is called a covalent (cō-vā'-lent) bond.

Bonds that are equally shared are *always* formed between two identical atoms like two hydrogens, two oxygens, two nitrogens, or two chlorine atoms.

However, covalent bonds also form between atoms that are *not* identical but still want to share electrons, like carbon and oxygen, carbon and hydrogen, and hydrogen and oxygen. The molecule formed by one carbon atom and four hydrogen atoms also has bonds with shared electrons and are covalent bonds.

A carbon atom and four hydrogens (CH_4) with shared electrons

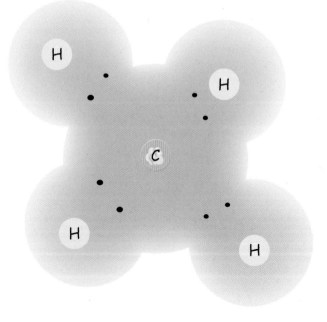

2.5 Unshared electron bonds

Sometimes the electrons are not shared between the two atoms. When this happens, one atom tends to want more electrons for itself and is not willing to share the electrons with the other atom. This results in a bond with *unshared* electrons. This type of bond is called an ionic (ī-o'-nik) bond.

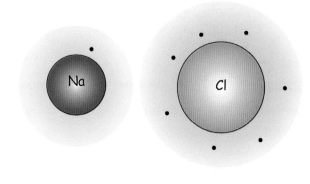

The sodium is missing an electron.

The chlorine has an extra electron.

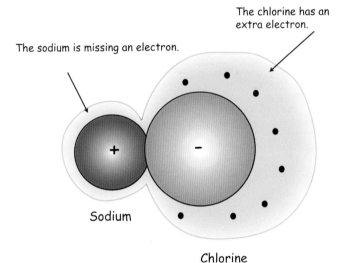

Sodium

Chlorine

The electrons in the bond between a sodium atom and chlorine atom are *not* shared. The sodium atom gives away one of its electrons to the chlorine atom. As a result, the sodium atom has fewer electrons than it would normally have if it were alone, and the chlorine atom has more electrons than it would normally have if it were alone.

The molecule formed by sodium and chlorine is called sodium (sō-dē-əm) chloride (klōr-īd). Sodium chloride is also known as "table salt."

We use table salt to flavor our food. The crystals that we sprinkle out are made of many, many molecules of sodium chloride packed together. The fact that the electrons are not shared in sodium chloride makes table salt very easy to dissolve in water (see Chapter 6), and this helps us taste it when we put it on our food.

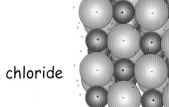

Sodium chloride crystal

2.6 Bonding rules

The number of electrons an atom has also determines *how many* bonds an atom can form. Atoms cannot form just any number of bonds with another atom.

For example, a hydrogen atom has only one electron, so it usually forms only one bond. Carbon, on the other hand, has a total of 6 electrons. However, only 4 of those electrons are available to make bonds, so carbon atoms usually form a total of 4 bonds. Nitrogen (nī'-trō-jen) has only three available electrons and usually forms three bonds. Oxygen (äk'-si-jen), with two available electrons, typically forms only two bonds.

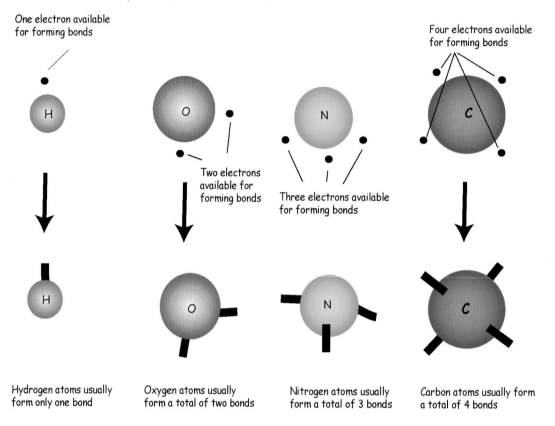

Hydrogen atoms usually form only one bond

Oxygen atoms usually form a total of two bonds

Nitrogen atoms usually form a total of 3 bonds

Carbon atoms usually form a total of 4 bonds

2.7 Shapes of molecules

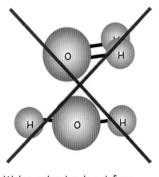

Water molecules do not form

All molecules have particular shapes. For example, when two hydrogen atoms bond with a single oxygen atom to make H_2O, or water, the molecules are bent. All water molecules are bent because of the way the electrons are arranged on the oxygen atom in a water molecule. This fact gives water special features that make it essential for all living things.

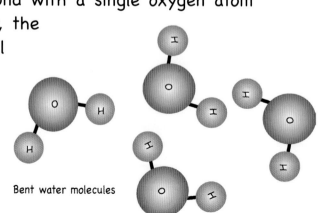

Bent water molecules

2.8 Summary

Here are the most important points to remember from this chapter:

- When two or more atoms combine, they form a molecule.

- Atoms in a molecule are "stuck" to each other with bonds.

- Bonds are formed with the electrons from each atom.

- Shared electron bonds are called covalent bonds.

- Unshared electron bonds are called ionic bonds.

- The number of bonds an atom can form depends on the number of available electrons.

- Molecules have certain shapes.

Chapter 3: Chemical Reactions

3.1 Introduction

What happens inside a battery? How does a car use gasoline to run? What happens to an egg when it's fried in a pan? All of these situations are examples of chemical reactions in action. Chemical reactions happen almost everywhere we look. They provide the energy that powers many things including cars, toys, plants, and animals. Our own bodies work by means of many complex chemical reactions.

A chemical reaction occurs whenever bonds between atoms and molecules are created or destroyed.

The following are four general types of chemical reactions:

1. Combination (käm-bə-nā'-shən) reactions occur when two or more molecules combine with each other to make a new molecule.

2. Decomposition (dē-käm-pō-zi'-shən) reactions occur when a molecule decomposes, or breaks apart, into two or more molecules.

3. Displacement reactions (dis-plās'-mənt) occur when one atom kicks another atom out of a molecule.

4. Exchange reactions (eks-chānj') occur when one atom trades places with another atom.

3.2 Combination reaction

In a combination reaction, two or more molecules combine to form a single product.

The reaction of sodium and chlorine to make sodium chloride, or table salt, is an example of a combination reaction. In this reaction two sodium atoms combine with one molecule of chlorine gas to make two molecules of sodium chloride.

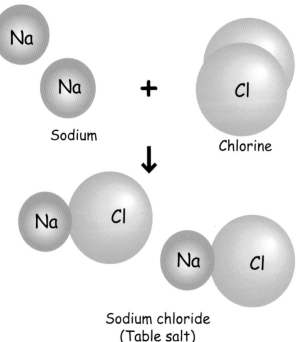

Sodium

Chlorine

Sodium chloride
(Table salt)

3.3 Decomposition reaction

In a decomposition reaction, molecules of one type break apart or *decompose* to make two or more products. The break up of water into hydrogen and oxygen gases is an example of a decomposition reaction.

3.4 Displacement reaction

A third general type of chemical reaction is the displacement reaction.

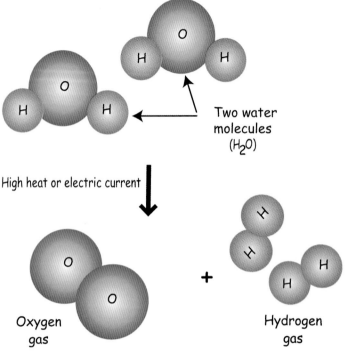

Two water molecules (H_2O)

High heat or electric current

Oxygen gas

+

Hydrogen gas

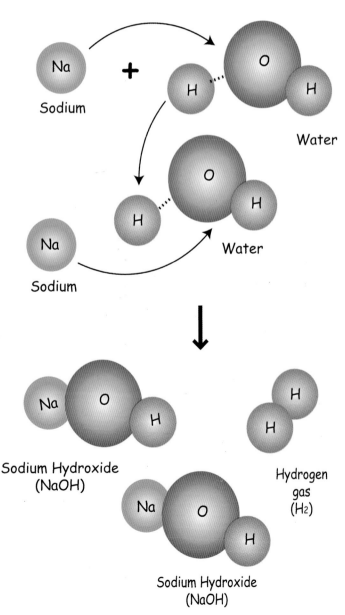

Sodium

Water

Sodium

Water

Sodium Hydroxide (NaOH)

Sodium Hydroxide (NaOH)

Hydrogen gas (H_2)

In this reaction, one atom will remove another atom from a compound to form a new product.

The formation of sodium hydroxide, by two water molecules and two metallic sodium atoms, is an example of a displacement reaction. The sodium atoms, labeled "Na" (shown as blue balls) kick out the hydrogen atoms, labeled "H" (shown as gray balls) from the water molecules. The sodium atoms combine with the remaining oxygen and hydrogen atom from the water molecule (called an hydroxide (hī-dräk'-sīd) ion) to make a new molecule called sodium hydroxide. The two hydrogen atoms that were kicked out by the sodium atoms form hydrogen gas.

3.5 Exchange reaction

The fourth type of general chemical reaction is the exchange reaction. In this reaction, the atoms of one molecule trade places with the atoms of another molecule to form two new molecules.

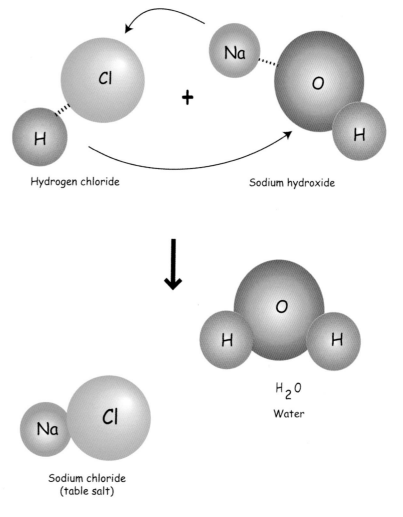

Hydrogen chloride

Sodium hydroxide

H_2O
Water

Sodium chloride
(table salt)

The reaction of hydrochloric acid (HCl) and sodium hydroxide (NaOH) is an example of an exchange reaction. The hydrogen atom in the HCl molecule trades places with the sodium atom in the NaOH molecule to make two new molecules, sodium chloride (table salt), and water.

These are the basic types of simple chemical reactions. Some reactions that have many components are much more complicated than those outlined in this chapter, but most chemical reactions fall into one of these four categories.

3.6 Spontaneous or not?

Not all chemical reactions are spontaneous (spän-tā'-nē-əs). Spontaneous means the reaction happens all by itself, by just mixing the chemicals. The reaction of hydrochloric acid (HCl) and sodium hydroxide (NaOH) (exchange reaction) is a spontaneous reaction. However, not all chemical reactions are spontaneous. The decomposition reaction of water into hydrogen gas and oxygen gas is *not* a spontaneous reaction. It requires either high heat or an electric current. It's a good thing that not all reactions occur spontaneously. Imagine how difficult it would be to swim or sail a boat, or even get a drink, if water spontaneously decomposed into hydrogen gas and oxygen gas!

3.7 Evidences of chemical reactions

To determine whether or not a chemical reaction has occurred, chemists look for certain signs, or evidences, of a change.

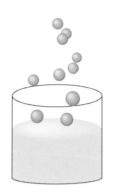

There are several signs that tell scientists when a chemical reaction has occured.

Bubbles forming

A chemist may look for bubbles being released when something gets added to something else. Bubbles indicate that a gas formed during the reaction.

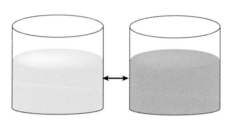

Or, if two solutions are mixed, one solution might change color.

Color change

Sometimes when two solutions are mixed, a temperature change occurs and the solution gets either hotter or colder.

Temperature change

Finally, another indication that a chemical reaction has taken place is the formation of a precipitate (prē-si'-pə-tāt), which can look like colored sand, mud, dust, or snow forming in a solution. A precipitate forms when the new molecules being made from the chemical reaction do not dissolve in the solution.

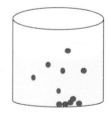

Precipitation

These are some of the ways that chemists can tell when a chemical reaction has taken place.

3.8 Summary

Here are the most important points to remember from this chapter:

- A chemical reaction occurs whenever bonds between atoms and molecules are created or destroyed.

- There are different kinds of chemical reactions. They are as follows:

   combination reactions where molecules join
   decomposition reactions where molecules break apart
   displacement reactions where molecules get removed
   exchange reactions where molecules trade places

- Not all chemical reactions occur spontaneously.

- Sometimes changes occur that indicate a chemical reaction has taken place. These changes include bubble formation, color changes, temperature changes, and precipitations.

Chapter 4: Acids, Bases, and pH

pH

0 1 2 3 4 5 6 7 8 9 10 11 12 13 14

4.1 Introduction

One very important type of chemical reaction is the acid-base reaction. Acid-base reactions are a very special kind of exchange reaction. Recall that in an exchange reaction, the atoms of one molecule trade places with the atoms of another molecule.

The chemical reaction of vinegar with baking soda is an acid-base reaction. Vinegar, or acetic acid, is an acid, and baking soda, or sodium bicarbonate, is a base. When vinegar and baking soda are mixed, one of the hydrogen atoms on the vinegar trades places with the sodium atom on the baking soda. This is a type of exchange reaction.

Acetic acid
(vinegar)
ACID

Sodium bicarbonate
(baking soda)
BASE

A hydrogen atom from the vinegar breaks away and replaces the sodium on the baking soda.

As we have already seen, when vinegar and baking soda are mixed together, bubbles are released. The bubbles are evidence that a chemical reaction has occurred.

4.2 The pH scale

Acids and bases have a special property that can be used to identify them. This property is called pH (pronounced "P" "H"). The pH is a measure of how acidic or how basic a solution is. The pH of pure water is 7. Pure water is neutral (nü'-trəl). If a substance is an acid and it is added to pure water, the pH will be LOWER than 7. If a substance is a base, adding it to pure water will RAISE the pH above 7.

> pH = 7: The solution is neither an acid nor a base, it is neutral.
> pH less than 7: The solution is an acid.
> pH more than 7: The solution is a base.

The next chart shows the pH of various solutions. Notice that the pH for blood is near 7, close to the pH of water. Our bodies are made of mostly water, and blood carries nutrients throughout our bodies. It is important that the pH of blood be near 7 since many of our cells and tissues would be damaged if the pH were much higher or much lower than 7. However, notice that the pH for stomach fluid is even lower than the pH for vinegar. Why is stomach fluid so acidic? As it turns out, your stomach is full of hydrochloric (hī-drō-klōr'-ik) acid , HCl. The acid helps to break down your food so that it can be carried to other places in your body. Your stomach has a special lining on the inside that is designed to prevent the acidic stomach fluid from causing damage.

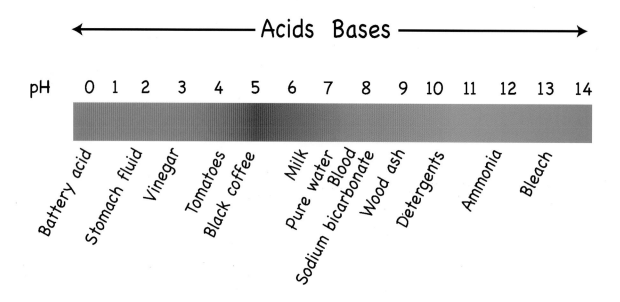

4.3 Properties of acids and bases

From the chart, some general properties of acids and bases can be determined. For example, vinegar, tomatoes, and black coffee are all acids and all have a sour taste. It turns out that most acids are sour tasting. Grapefruit, for example, is not on the chart, but it is very sour. The juice inside a grapefruit contains a lot of citric (si'-trik) acid. Detergents and many cleaners feel slippery. This is because many cleaners are basic, and slipperiness tends to be a property of bases.

General Properties	
Acids	Bases
sour in taste	bitter in taste
not slippery to touch	slippery to touch
dissolve metals	react with metals to form precipitates

Some acids and bases are very poisonous or corrosive and can easily harm you. Battery acid, for example, can burn your skin if it happens to spill. It can also make you very sick if eaten.

4.4 Measuring pH

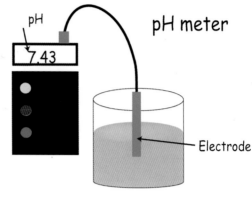

pH meter

A better way to tell if something is an acid or a base is the pH. The pH of a solution can be measured in a variety of ways.

One way is to use a pH meter. A pH meter is a device that measures the pH directly. A small stick, called an electrode (ē-lek'-trōd), is placed into the solution, and the pH is read directly from the meter.

Another way to measure pH is to use pH paper. pH paper is special paper that changes color when placed in either an acid or a base. Litmus paper is a very common type of pH paper. If blue litmus paper is placed in an acidic solution, the paper turns red. If red litmus paper is placed in a basic solution, the paper turns blue.

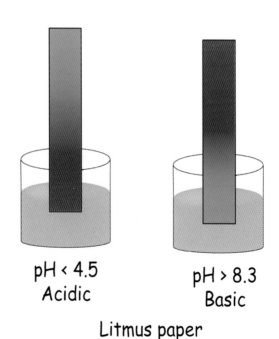

pH < 4.5
Acidic

pH > 8.3
Basic

Litmus paper

Litmus paper has special chemicals absorbed into the fiber of the paper. These chemicals are called acid-base indicators. The indicator that is in litmus paper is a natural dye that comes from lichens (a type of tree moss). Indicators are usually organic molecules (molecules made up of mostly carbon, hydrogen, and oxygen), and the color of these chemicals depends on the pH of the solution.

There are different kinds of acid-base indicators. Some indicators change colors at very low pH and others don't change until the pH is very high. Some indicators even change colors twice. The the next chart shows a few acid-base indicators and the pH range in which they change color.

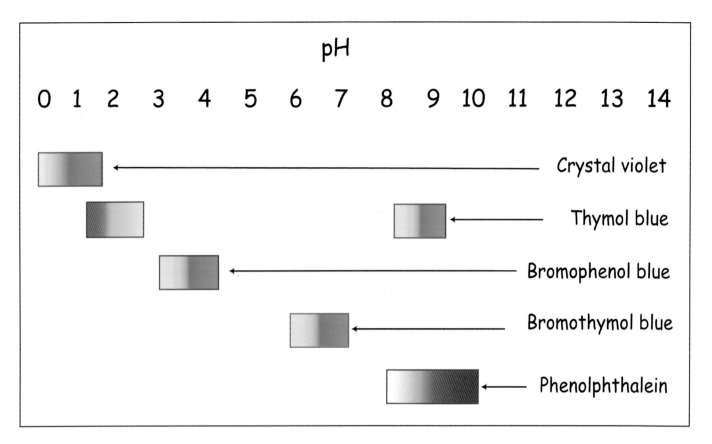

From the chart, we can see that crystal violet changes colors at very low pH. Below pH 1 crystal violet is yellow, but above pH 1 it is blue. Now look at phenolphthalein (fē-nōl-thā'-lēn). Below pH 9 phenolphthalein is not colored, but above pH 9 it turns pink. pH indicators are very useful for finding the pH of a solution and determining whether it is an acid or a base.

In general, any molecule that changes color when the pH changes can be considered an acid-base indicator. There are many different acid-base indicators.

4.5 Summary

Here are the most important points to remember from this chapter:

° Acids and bases react with each other in a special kind of exchange reaction.

° The pH tells whether a solution is an acid or a base.

° pH can be measured by pH meters, pH paper, and indicators.

Chapter 5: Acid-Base Neutralization

5.1 Introduction

When an acid is added to a base or a base is added to an acid, a chemical reaction occurs. We saw this earlier with the reaction between vinegar (an acid) and baking soda (a base). Recall that an acid-base reaction is called an exchange reaction because the atoms (ions) in one molecule trade places with the atoms (ions) in the other molecule.

An acid-base reaction is also called a neutralization (nü-trə-lī-zā'-shən) reaction. When an acid reacts with a base, the atoms that make the acid acidic (hydrogen ions) react with the atoms that make the base basic (hydroxyl ions) to form water and salt. When this happens, the acid and base neutralize (nü'-trə-līz) each other.

The reaction of acetic acid and sodium bicarbonate is actually a combination of two reactions. The initial step is the acid-base portion of the reaction, where the hydrogen ion on the acid trades places with the sodium ion on the base. The next step is a decomposition reaction, where carbon dioxide is produced and released as bubbles.

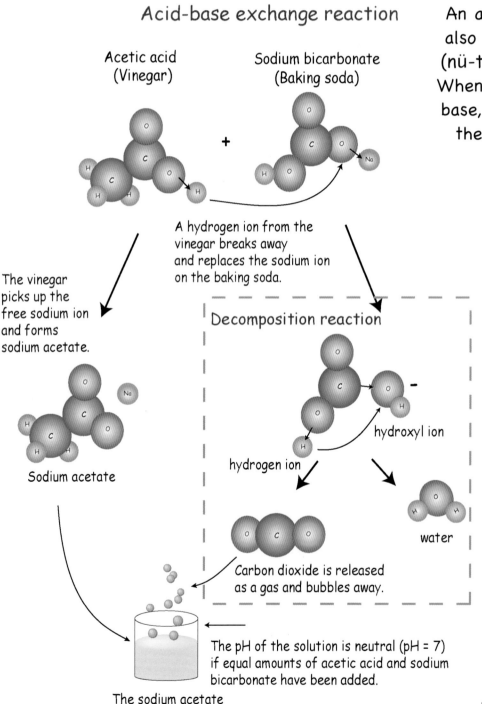

Acid-base exchange reaction

Acetic acid
(Vinegar)

Sodium bicarbonate
(Baking soda)

A hydrogen ion from the vinegar breaks away and replaces the sodium ion on the baking soda.

The vinegar picks up the free sodium ion and forms sodium acetate.

Sodium acetate

Decomposition reaction

hydroxyl ion

hydrogen ion

water

Carbon dioxide is released as a gas and bubbles away.

The pH of the solution is neutral (pH = 7) if equal amounts of acetic acid and sodium bicarbonate have been added.

The sodium acetate stays in the solution dissolved in the water.

When equal amounts of acid react with equal amounts of base, both the acid and the base are neutralized. In the case of vinegar and baking soda, the acid was turned into a salt and the baking soda was converted into carbon dioxide and water. The carbon dioxide went away as bubbles, and the salt and water stayed in the jar.

5.2 Concentration

The fact that equal amounts of acids and bases can neutralize each other is very useful for chemists. Sometimes chemists are very concerned with *how much* of something they have. More precisely, they want to know how many molecules they might have in a given volume of solution. You can see that if you have more acid molecules in one solution than in another, it will be more acidic.

The number of molecules in a given volume of solution is called the concentration (kän-sen-trā'-shən). If there are a lot of molecules in a solution, then it is concentrated. If there are fewer molecules, then the solution is dilute (dī-loot').

In the laboratory, concentrated (pure) acetic acid is called glacial (glā-shəl) acetic (ə-sē'-tik) acid. It has a very strong odor, and bottles of it must be opened in a special place called a fume hood. It would badly burn you if spilled on your skin. However, dilute acetic acid is vinegar. It is the same acid, but much less concentrated and, therefore, OK (and delicious) to eat on a salad.

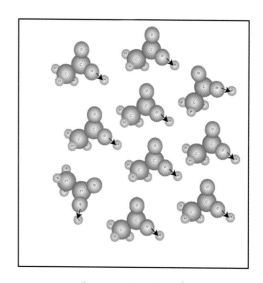

Concentrated
acetic acid

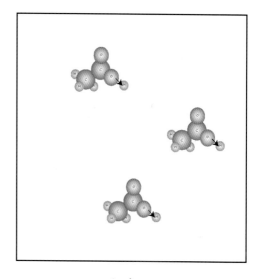

Dilute
acetic acid

Sometimes it may be necessary to neutralize an acid with a base or a base with an acid. For example, when someone eats too many chili cheese fries he or she might suffer from indigestion. When a person has indigestion, the acid inside his or her stomach causes pain. A good way to reduce that pain is to neutralize the acid. There are many different "antacids" that are used to neutralize stomach acid. All antacids are bases, and when someone uses an antacid his or her stomach acid is neutralized. Antacids are not very strong or concentrated, so they are safe to eat.

5.3 Titration

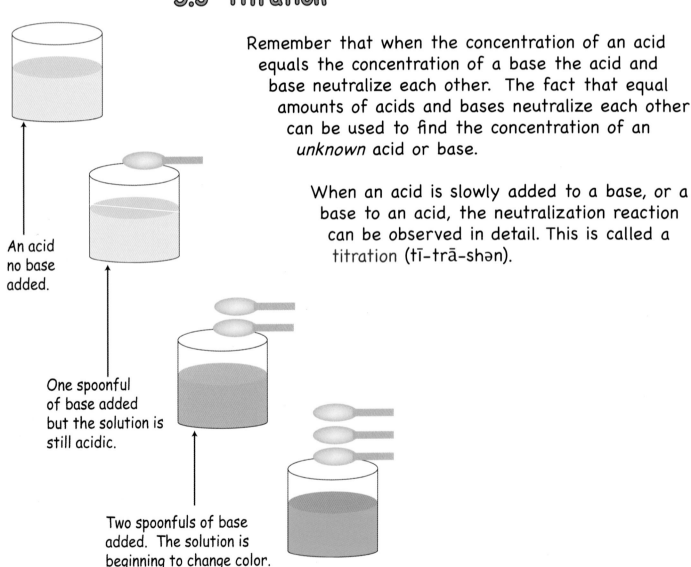

Remember that when the concentration of an acid equals the concentration of a base the acid and base neutralize each other. The fact that equal amounts of acids and bases neutralize each other can be used to find the concentration of an *unknown* acid or base.

When an acid is slowly added to a base, or a base to an acid, the neutralization reaction can be observed in detail. This is called a titration (tī-trā-shən).

An acid no base added.

One spoonful of base added but the solution is still acidic.

Two spoonfuls of base added. The solution is beginning to change color.

With three spoonfuls of base added, the acid has been neutralized. ⟶ If the concentration of the base is known, the concentration of the acid can be determined from this titration.

5.4 Plotting data

One way to examine the titration in detail is to *plot or graph* the data. A plot is a handy tool that scientists use to understand data. Plots can be made of almost anything. For example, you might notice that the older members in your family are usually taller than the younger members. So, you could say that there is a connection between *age* and *height*. A plot can be made to illustrate the relationship between age and height. To make a plot of age vs. (versus) height, a line is drawn horizontally on the paper. Another line is drawn perpendicular to the first, or vertically, and crosses over the first line on the left-hand side. These two lines are called axes; each one is called an axis. To plot age vs. height, the bottom axis is labeled "age" and the vertical axis is labeled "height." Now, data can be collected and it might look something like this:

Age	Height
age 1	2 ft
age 6	3 ft
age 8	4 ft
age 11	5 ft
age 30	5 1/2 ft
age 40	5 3/4 ft
age 60	5 4/5 ft

To plot the data, the age of the person is marked on the graph with a vertical dotted line. Then, the height of the person is marked with a horizontal dotted line and the point where the two lines intersect is marked with a red dot. A solid black line can be drawn to connect all of the red dots (points) on the plot.

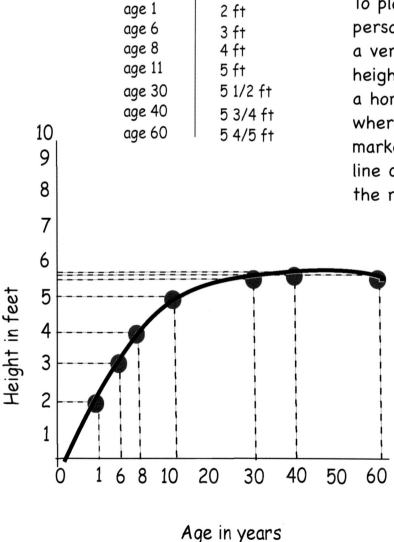

From the plot we can tell that, in general, as a person gets older, he or she grows taller. (The solid black line goes up as the age goes up.) The graph also shows that a person stops growing when he or she reaches a certain age. (The solid black line levels off, showing that no significant growth occurs after age 20 or so.) Plotting is a tool that scientists use to organize their data so that it is easier to understand.

Age in years

5.5 Plot of an acid-base titration

A plot of an acid-base titration has a horizontal axis labeled "Amount of base (or acid) added," and a vertical axis labeled "pH" or "color." A titration of a base into an acid may look something like this:

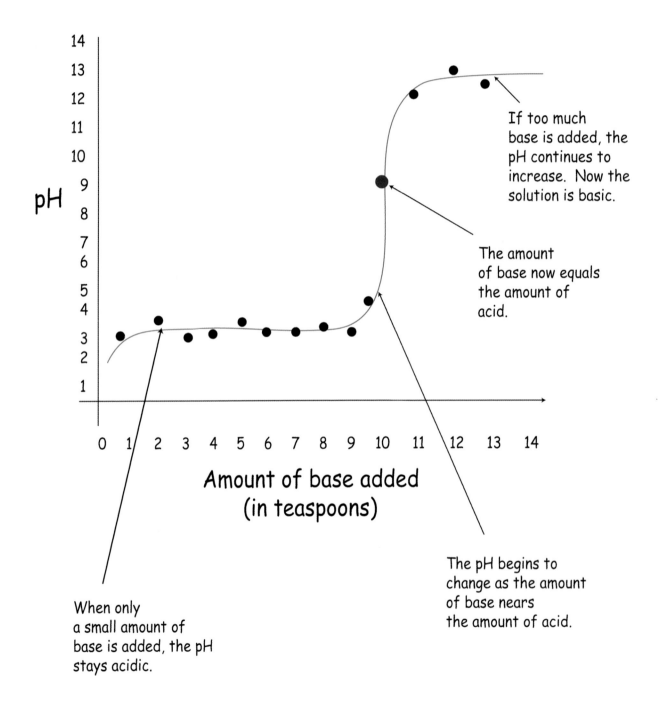

If too much base is added, the pH continues to increase. Now the solution is basic.

The amount of base now equals the amount of acid.

The pH begins to change as the amount of base nears the amount of acid.

When only a small amount of base is added, the pH stays acidic.

pH

Amount of base added (in teaspoons)

By doing a titration, the chemist can determine the concentration of an unknown acid or base.

5.6 Summary

Here are the most important points to remember from this chapter:

° An acid and a base neutralize each other in an acid-base reaction.

° Equal amounts of acid and base completely neutralize each other.

° The concentration of an unknown acid or base can be found using a titration.

Chapter 6: Mixtures

6.1 Introduction

Sometimes things that look like they are made up of only one item are really made of many items. For example, when we eat cake we may think that we are eating only cake, but cake has many different ingredients in it. It has flour, eggs, butter, maybe some salt, water or milk, baking powder, and, hopefully chocolate.

Cake is really a mixture of many ingredients:

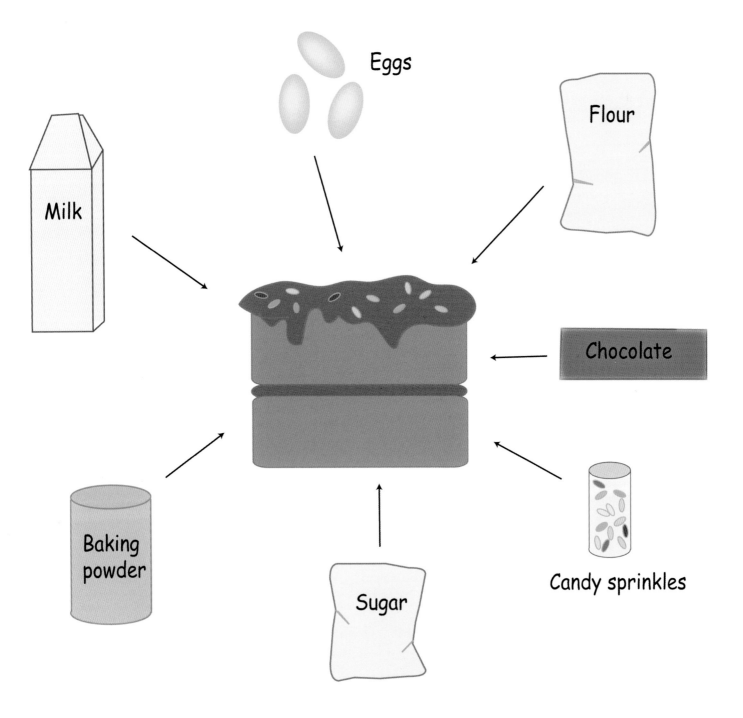

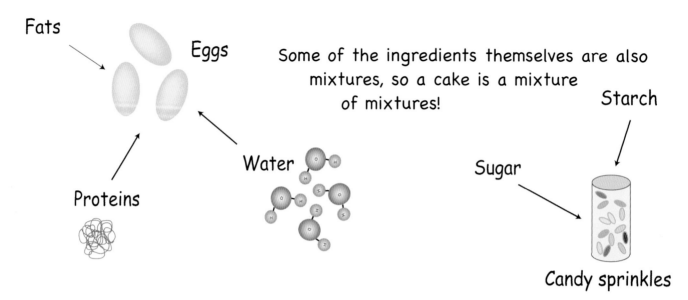

Fats

Eggs

Proteins

Water

Some of the ingredients themselves are also mixtures, so a cake is a mixture of mixtures!

Starch

Sugar

Candy sprinkles

6.2 Types of mixtures

There are two main types of mixtures called homogeneous (hō-mō-jē′-nē-əs) and heterogeneous (he-tə-rō′-jē′-nē-əs) mixtures.

Homo comes from the Greek word *homos* which means "the same," and geneous comes from the Greek word *genos* which means "kind." So a homogeneous mixture is a mixture of the "same kind." An example of a homogeneous mixture is salt water. In a glass of salt water, the salt water is the same everywhere in the glass. The top of the glass does not have different salt water than the bottom of the glass, so salt water is considered a *homogeneous mixture*.

The salt is the same everywhere.

Salt water is a homogeneous mixture.

More ice cubes at the top than at the bottom.

Ice water is a heterogeneous mixture.

Hetero comes from the Greek word heteros which means "other" so a heterogeneous mixture is a mixture of "other kind." An example of a heterogeneous mixture is ice water. Although ice and water are both water, ice has different properties than water. Ice floats in water. In a glass of ice water there will be more ice at the top of the glass than at the bottom of the glass. The mixture of ice and water is not the same throughout, so it is called a *heterogeneous mixture*.

6.3 Like dissolves like

Homogeneous mixtures are made of substances that like to mix. When salt is added to water, the water molecules break apart the salt crystals into sodium ions and chloride ions. The salt is said to dissolve or "break apart" in the water. When this happens a homogeneous saltwater mixture is created.

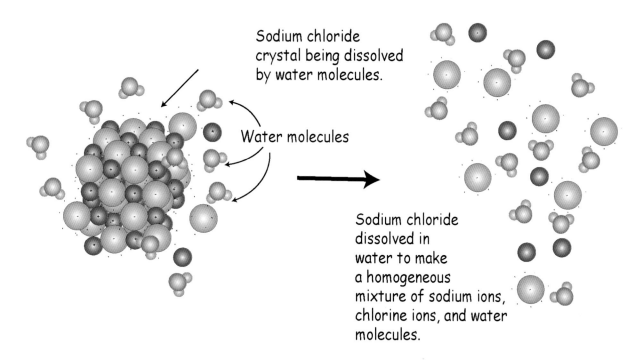

Sodium chloride crystal being dissolved by water molecules.

Water molecules

Sodium chloride dissolved in water to make a homogeneous mixture of sodium ions, chlorine ions, and water molecules.

Two substances that do not like to mix make heterogeneous mixtures. For example, when oil is added to water the oil stays in little droplets or floats to the top. No matter how hard these two are shaken, they simply do not mix.

Why does salt dissolve in water and not oil? As it turns out, the properties of the individual molecules determine if something will dissolve or not. The rule is:

Like dissolves like.

This simply means that molecules that are like each other will dissolve in each other, and molecules that are not alike will not dissolve in each other.

Salt and water are alike, in some ways, and oil and water are not.

Water molecules and salt molecules are alike in that they both have charged parts. Recall that the bond for a sodium chloride molecule is an ionic bond. Ionic bonds are easy to pull apart. When this happens the chlorine *ions* and the sodium *ions* are charged. Water molecules can easily pull apart the sodium and chloride bonds because water is positively charged on one end and negatively charged on the other end.

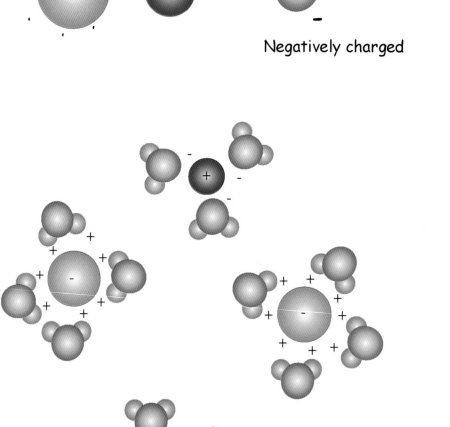

Positively charged

Negatively charged

The bonds holding the water molecules do not break apart because the bonds in a water molecule are not ionic bonds but are covalent bonds. (See Chapter 2). Instead, the charged ends of the water molecules surround the free sodium and free chloride ions.

Charged ends of water molecules surrounding the

Note that the negative ends of the water molecules surround the positive sodium ions, and the positive ends of the water molecules surround the negative chloride ions. The fact that both the water molecules and the salt molecules are "alike" in certain chemical ways because they are both charged, one will *dissolve* in the other.

Oil molecules, on the other hand, are not charged. Oil molecules are long chains of hydrogen and carbon atoms hooked together, and they do not carry any effective charge.

The molecule that makes up vegetable oil, glycerol (gli-sə-rol) trioleate (trī-ō-lē-āt), is made of three long chains of carbons and hydrogens connected together on one end. This molecule has no charged parts; therefore, it is not *like* water and cannot mix with or dissolve in water. However, it can be dissolved in other molecules that are also not charged, like mineral oil (octadecane) or even gasoline!

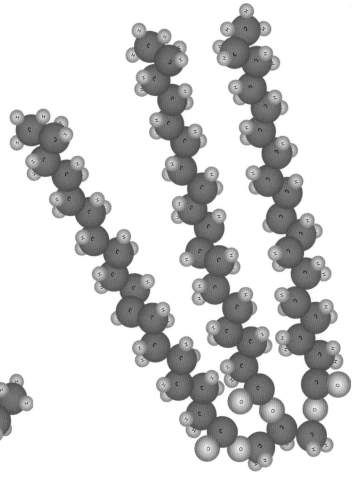

Glycerol trioleate
(vegetable oil)

Octadecane
(mineral oil)

The principle that like dissolves like can be used to decide how something might be cleaned. For example, those things that dissolve in water, like ammonia, bleach, and water-based paints, can be cleaned with water. However, those things that do not dissolve in water, like grease and oil-based paints, cannot be cleaned with water. Many cleaning fluids, like mineral spirits, are made of molecules that are not charged and can, therefore, dissolve oil-based paints or grease.

6.4 Soap

Mineral spirits and gasoline, although effective on grease, are not very useful for washing away olive oil from your hands after preparing salad. Also, these solutions are very poisonous and can easily catch on fire. So what can be used instead?

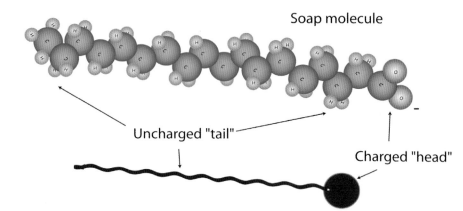

Soap molecule

Uncharged "tail"

Charged "head"

Soap, of course! Soaps are molecules that have both a charged end *and* an uncharged end. These molecules are able to dissolve oil in water because they have an *uncharged* part (that likes oil) and a *charged* part (that likes water).

When soap comes into contact with an oil molecule, the uncharged part (or oily part) mixes with the oil. The charged part of the soap molecule does not want to mix with the oil, so it stays mixed with the water. This results in very tiny droplets called micelles (mī-cel'). Inside a micelle the greasy end of the

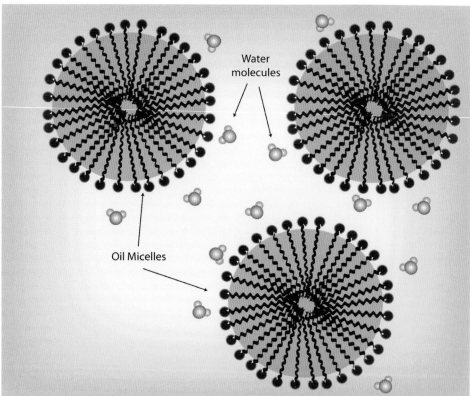

Water molecules

Oil Micelles

soap is dissolved in the oil and the charged end is dissolved in the water on the outside. These tiny droplets can then be washed away with the water.

6.5 Summary

Here are the most important points to remember from this chapter:

° There are two types of mixtures: homogeneous and heterogeneous.

° Homogeneous mixtures are made by things that are "like" each other.

° Heterogenous mixtures are made by things that are "not like" each other.

° Things that are "alike" dissolve in each other: *Like dissolves like.*

° Soap helps oil "dissolve" in water.

Chapter 7: Separating Mixtures

7.1 Introduction

Sometimes mixtures are desirable and result in tasty cakes, refreshing Kool-Aid, and clean hands, but other times mixtures need to be separated. For example, when boiling spaghetti noodles, the mixture of spaghetti and hot water

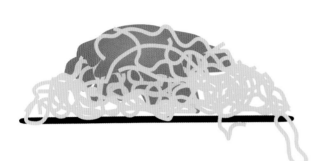

first needs to be separated before sauce can be added. To do this, the spaghetti is placed in a sieve or colander. The water runs through the small holes of the sieve, but the spaghetti is retained because it is too large. This is a simple example of separation. Separation is the process of removing one or more items from a mixture.

7.2 Filtration

Separating spaghetti noodles from water is called filtration (fil-trā′-shən). Filtration can be used to separate two or more things of different size. Since the spaghetti noodles are much larger than the water molecules, it is easy to separate them with a sieve. A sieve is a kind of filter. The holes in a filter are called pores. The size of the pores in a filter determines the size of things that can be separated. Large pores, like in the sieve, separate large things, like spaghetti, from smaller things like water. Filters with small pores can separate small molecules from large molecules. The smaller the pore size, the smaller the molecule that can be separated.

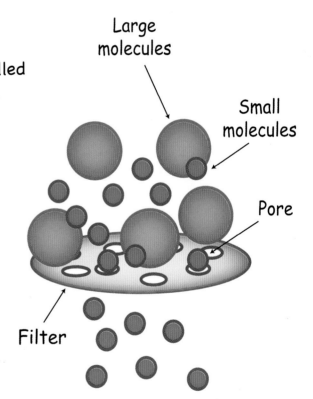

Large molecules

Small molecules

Pore

Filter

7.3 Evaporation

Filtration cannot be used to separate items of the same size. For example, spaghetti noodles cannot be separated from linguine noodles with a sieve since they are nearly the same size. Likewise, salt molecules cannot be separated from water molecules by filtration since they are also nearly the same size.

So just how does one separate salt molecules from water molecules? One way is by using a different technique called evaporation (ē-vap-ō-rā'-shən). When water is allowed to evaporate, the salt gets left behind as a solid.

7.4 Solids, liquids, and gases

Many molecules, like water, exist in three different *states*. These states are the solid state (ice for water), the liquid state (liquid water), and the gaseous state (steam). We know that, if an ice cube is placed into a hot pan it begins to melt and eventually disappears. What happened? Did the water vanish and cease to be water? No, the water simply changed from the solid state (ice) to the liquid state (water) to the gaseous state (water vapor). It *disappears* because our eyes cannot see the tiny water molecules as a gas.

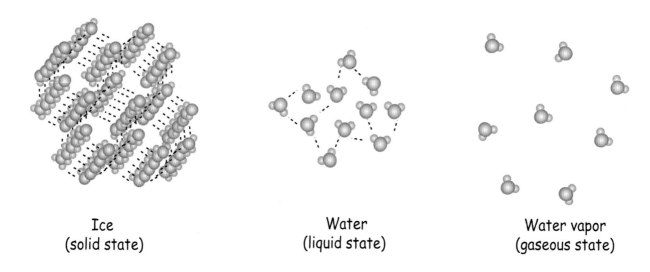

| Ice | Water | Water vapor |
| (solid state) | (liquid state) | (gaseous state) |

Water molecules like to "stick" to each other. This causes the molecules to form ice and liquid water. When heat is applied, the ice cube melts because the heat is adding "energy" to the molecules. This energy causes the molecules to move faster and faster. Soon the molecules are moving so fast they cannot stick to each other as well. Eventually the molecules have enough energy to completely break away from each other and become a gas.

Even without added heat, water molecules can still turn into a gas, but they do it more slowly. This is called evaporation. To separate water from salt molecules by evaporation, the water slowly turns into a gas and floats away. We say that the water has evaporated leaving the salt molecules behind.

7.5 Chromatography

What if the molecules can't be separated by evaporation?

Another technique used to separate mixtures is chromatography (krō-mə-tä'-grə-fē). Chromatography relies on the fact that different molecules stick to each other in different ways. Chromato comes from the Greek word *chroma*, which means "color," and graphy comes from the Greek word *graphe,* which means "to write." So chromatography means "to write with color." This technique is so named because chromatography was originally used to separate colored compounds. Today, however, chromatography is used to separate substances of all kinds.

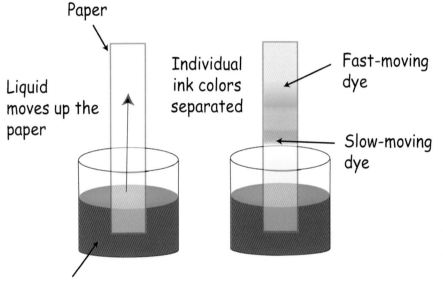

Paper

Liquid moves up the paper

Individual ink colors separated

Fast-moving dye

Slow-moving dye

Alcohol-ink mixture

The simplest form of chromatography can be carried out by just standing a strip of paper in a solution. This is called paper chromatography. Because different molecules stick to paper in different ways, the molecules can be separated. For example, ink is usually a mixture of several dye molecules of different colors. The individual colors in ink can be separated from each other by using paper chromatography. To do this, the ink is dissolved in alcohol, or some other solvent, and one end of a thin strip of paper is dipped into the ink-alcohol mixture. The alcohol will begin to creep up the paper and carry the dye molecules with it. The different colors in the ink stick to the paper differently, so they move up at different rates. Soon all of the colors in the ink are separated.

There are other kinds of chromatography, like gas chromatography where different gas molecules are separated from each other. However, all types of chromatography operate on similar principles.

7.6 Summary

Here are the most important points to remember from this chapter:

○ Mixtures can be separated using several methods including filtration, evaporation, and chromatography.

○ Filtration is used to separate smaller things from larger things.

○ Evaporation can be used to separate molecules that evaporate from molecules that don't evaporate.

○ Paper chromatography can be used to separate different colors in ink.

○ There are three states of matter: solids, liquids, and gases. The molecules in a solid are closer together than the molecules in a liquid. In a gas, the molecules are far apart from each other.

Chapter 8: Energy Molecules

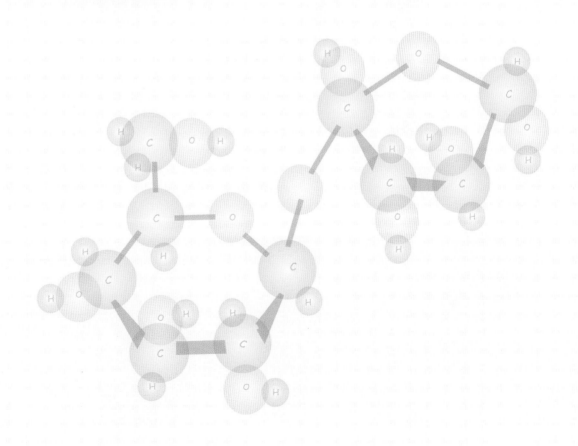

8.1 Introduction

Have you ever wondered why we need to eat food? We may know from experience that when we skip a meal or are unable to eat because of illness, we become weak and lack energy. Our bodies require food to help us grow and keep our "engines running." Without food we would not survive.

Unlike plants, we cannot stick our feet in the soil, lift our hands to the sun, and make our own food. In fact, we rely on plants and other animals to provide the food our bodies need to keep us going. But what is in food and what does it do for us?

8.2 Nutrients

There are many different kinds of nutrients our bodies require to stay healthy. These include vitamins, proteins (prō-tēns), fats, and carbohydrates (kär-bō-hī'-drāts) We get these important nutrients from eating a variety of foods. The nutrients we get from eating foods provide the necessary molecules our bodies need to grow and function properly. Vitamins, like those found in carrots, help our eyes to work. Fats found in vegetable oil and butter help our brains and other tissues to function. Proteins from fish and meats help our bones to heal and our muscles to grow. Carbohydrates, like those found in bread, potatoes, and sweets, provide us with "energy."

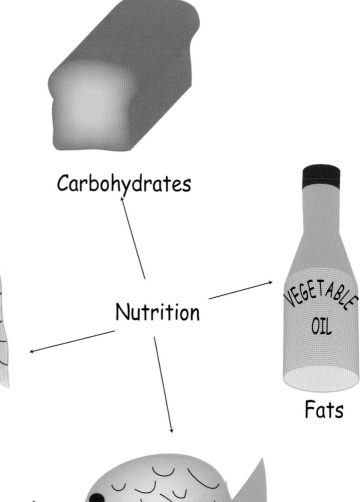

Carbohydrates

Nutrition

Vitamins

Fats

Proteins

8.3 Carbohydrates

What are carbohydrates and how do they provide energy for our bodies?

The name "carbohydrate" is a general term for many different kinds of molecules that contain carbon, oxygen, and hydrogen. Carbo means "carbon" and hydrate means "water," so carbohydrate means "a combination of carbon and water."

The simplest carbohydrates are the sugars. Sugars are relatively small molecules. They taste sweet and can be easily broken down by our bodies to provide quick energy. The very simplest sugars are called monosaccharides (mä-nō-sa'-kə-rīd). *Mono* comes from the Greek language and means "single," and saccharide (sa'-kə-rīd) means "sugar," so a monosaccharide is a "single sugar." The single sugars, glucose and fructose, are monosaccharides.

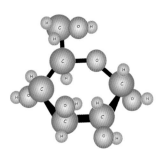

Glucose
a simple sugar

Fructose
a simple sugar

When a few monosaccharides are put together, they are called oligosaccharides (ō-li-gō-sa-kə-rīd). *Oligo* is Greek for "a few," so an oligosaccharide is a "few sugars." Sucrose is an example of an oligosaccharide. Sucrose is a single molecule of glucose (glü'-cōs) hooked to a single molecule of fructose (frük'-tōs) by a chemical bond. Sucrose is common table sugar; the same sugar that we buy in the store and put on strawberries.

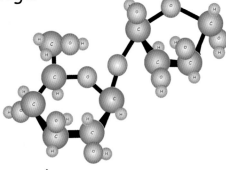

Sucrose
glucose + fructose

Sugar

8.4 Starches

When more than a few saccharides, or sugars, are hooked together the molecule is called a polysaccharide (po-lē-sa'-kə-rīd). *Poly* means "many" so a polysaccharide means "many sugars." Polysaccharide molecules usually contain ten or more monosaccharides.

There are two general types of polysaccharides called starch and cellulose (sel'-yoo-lōs). Starches are the molecules that provide our bodies with most of the energy we need to live and work. Potatoes, pasta, and bread are excellent sources of starches.

There are three main kinds of starches. Glycogen (glī'-kə-jən) is a starch that animals produce in their livers and store in their muscles. Amylose (a'-mi-lōs) and Amylopectin (a-mi-lō-pek'-tin) are two starches that are made by plants and are the main energy-storage molecules found in rice and potatoes.

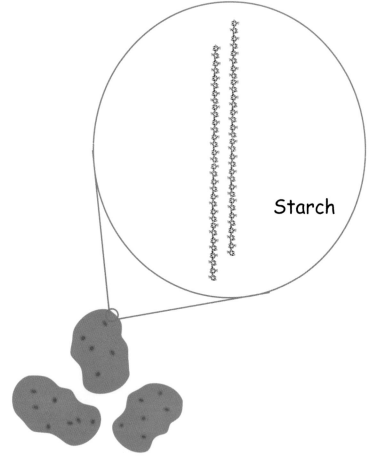

Starch

All of these polysaccharides are composed of only glucose molecules linked together to make long chains. They can have as many as 3000 glucose units hooked together in a row.

So how do our bodies use these long chains of glucose for energy? We have special proteins in our bodies that break the long chains up into individual glucose molecules. The single glucose molecules are used directly by our bodies for energy. So if it is only the glucose our bodies

Potatoes

need, why not eat only the simple sugars and have a diet rich in candy-coated sugar bomb cereal?

If we ate only simple sugars, our bodies would use up all of the energy in these molecules too quickly and we would get tired. The long chains in the polysaccharides provide "storage" for the energy molecules so that we will have enough energy to ride bikes, swim, or run.

8.5 Cellulose

Cellulose differs from the starches only in how the glucose molecules are hooked together. The links between the glucose molecules in cellulose are different from the links between those of the starches. For the starches, the oxygen atom that connects the two glucose molecules is pointing "down." However, the oxygen between the two glucose molecules in cellulose is pointing "up." The direction of this bond is the only difference between these two molecules, but it makes a huge difference to us.

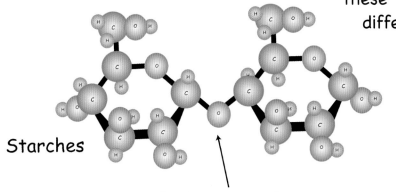

Starches

Links between glucoses

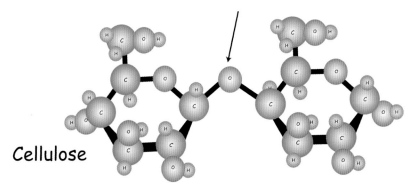

Cellulose

Cellulose is the main ingredient of wood, cotton, flax, wood pulp, and other plant fibers. It is even in grass. However, wood and grass are not main staples of our diet and not often served for Sunday brunch. In fact, although cellulose has the same glucose molecules that the starches have, humans cannot use cellulose for food energy at all.

Many animals, including humans, do not have the enzyme (protein) required to break the bonds between the glucose molecules in cellulose. Our enzymes only recognize the bonds in the starches; so we cannot graze the lawn for breakfast. Some animals, like cattle and horses, have bacteria that provide the necessary enzymes to break cellulose links, so these animals can eat grass for food energy, but we cannot.

8.6 Summary

Here are the most important points to remember from this chapter:

- Carbohydrates are molecules that give our bodies energy.

- Simple carbohydrates are sugars and larger carbohydrates are starches and cellulose.

- Our bodies cannot use cellulose for energy because we cannot break the bonds in a cellulose molecule. Animals, such as horses and cows, can eat grass for food because they have bacteria that can break the bonds in a cellulose molecule.

Chapter 9: Polymers

9.1 Introduction

In the last chapter we saw that energy molecules are very long chains of single sugars. Polysaccharides are one kind of molecule in a class of molecules called polymers (po'-li-mər). Recall that *poly* means "many." Mers comes from the Greek word *meros* which means "a part" or "unit," so a polymer is "many parts or units." Simply put, polymers are large-chain molecules made up of many, smaller, repeating units.

Polymers, both natural and synthetic, play a critical role in our everyday lives. Everywhere we look, we are likely to run into polymers.

Plastic, cloth, and rubber, are all polymers. This means that football helmets, car tires, hoola hoops, yo-yos, volleyball nets, and volleyballs are all made of polymers.

9.2 Polymer uses

Polymers are used for pipes that bring clean water into our homes. Polymers are used for clothing and packaging, in hospitals and under the ocean. Polymers are indispensible in the modern world. Also, the most important molecules in our bodies are polymers, as we will see in the next chapter.

Some polymers are soft and some are very hard. Some polymers are stretchable and some are very stiff. What makes polymers so different? How can they have so many uses and so many different properties if they are only strings of small molecules?

9.3 Structure of polymers

Polymers are so different from each other because there are so many different ways to make polymers. A polymer is just a chain of smaller molecules called monomers. Recall that *mono* means "one" so a monomer is "one unit." Polymers can be made of only one kind of monomer unit, like the starches and cellulose, or they can be made of different monomer units (like proteins and DNA; see next chapter). There are lots of different kinds of molecules that will form polymers.

For example, one common polymer that makes most plastics is called polyethylene (pä-lē-e'-thə-lēn). Polyethylene chains are very simple chemically, just carbons and hydrogens. Polymers can be single chains or they can have branches or side chains. They can be tightly packed or they can be loosely packed. These differences give them some of their different properties.

polyethylene chain with loosely packed side branches.

polyethylene chain closely packed with no side branches.

When the monomers for polyethylene are closely packed the plastic is very hard. This plastic is used to make bottle caps, toys, sewer pipes, and the casing around electronic equipment such as TVs and radios. However, when polyethylene molecules are loosely packed the plastic is much softer. This softer form of polyethylene is used to make plastic bags, squeeze bottles, plastic wrap for food, and other items. Both types of plastic have exactly the same kinds of molecules, but they differ in the way they are packed together.

9.4 Modifying polymers

In addition, polymer properties can change if single polymer molecules are connected to other single polymer molecules.

Polymer molecules sliding past one another

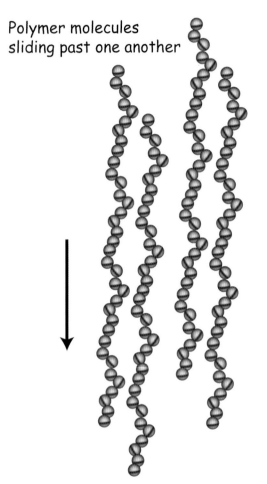

Natural rubber

For example, natural rubber is very soft and sticky when it is hot. It is not very useful for making tires and kitchen gloves because it is too soft and sticky. However, if natural rubber is heated with sulfur, it becomes harder and not sticky. This process is called vulcanization (vul-kə-nī-zā´-shən).

How does this work? The polymers in natural rubber are single chains and can easily slip past one another. This makes the rubber soft and sticky.

When natural rubber is heated to high temperatures with sulfur, the individual polymers become hooked together by sulfur bonds. This makes the rubber harder and easier to mold into things like tires or kitchen gloves.

Vulcanization is a way of making cross-links between individual polymer chains. These cross-links change the properties of the rubber.

Polymer molecules cannot slide past each other because of sulfur bonds

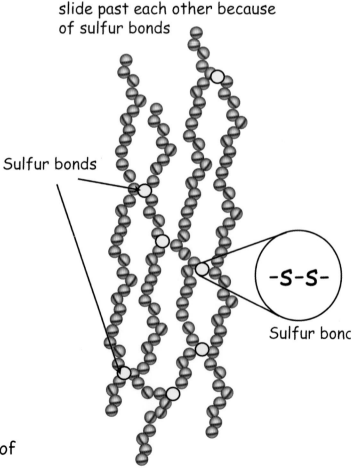

Sulfur bonds

-S-S-

Sulfur bond

Vulcanized rubber

9.5 Summary

Here are the most important points to remember from this chapter:

○ Polymers are long chains made of many repeating units. Carbohydrates are a kind of polymer. Plastics are also made of polymers.

○ Polymers can have different shapes. They can be long chains or they may have side branches. The different shapes give polymers different properties like whether they are hard or soft.

○ Polymers can be modified, or changed, with chemicals or heat. The vulcanization of natural rubber to make it harder is an example of modifying a polymer.

Chapter 10: Biological Polymers
Proteins and DNA

10.1 Introduction

There are two very important polymers that all living things contain: proteins (prō'-tēn) and DNA (say "D" "N" "A"). Proteins and DNA are biological polymers because they are found in biological organisms. Without proteins and DNA, life as we know it would not be possible.

10.2 Proteins

Proteins are polymers of amino (ə-mē'-nō) acids. An amino acid is a carbon atom with a carboxylic (kär-bäk-si'-lic) acid group and an amine (ə'-mēn) group attached. A carboxylic acid group is simply a carbon atom with two oxygens and one hydrogen. An amine group is a nitrogen atom with two hydrogens. Both of these groups are attached to a central carbon atom, which is called the "α" (alpha (al-fə))

Amino acid

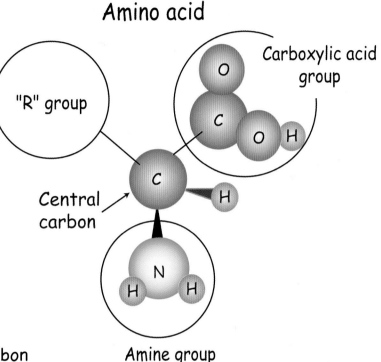

"R" group

Carboxylic acid group

Central carbon

Amine group

carbon.

All amino acids have this basic structure, but not all amino acids are the same. There are 20 different amino acids commonly found in proteins. What makes each amino acid different is the "R" group. The "R" group can be a single atom like hydrogen (as in glycine), or it can be a collection of atoms as in alanine (al-ə-nēn). The "R" group is different for each amino acid and gives each amino acid its own special properties.

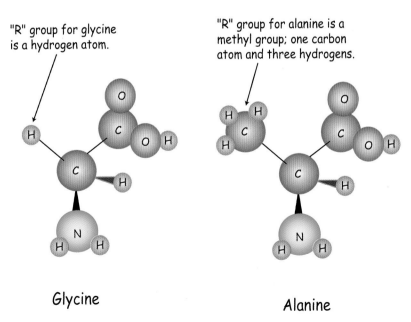

"R" group for glycine is a hydrogen atom.

"R" group for alanine is a methyl group; one carbon atom and three hydrogens.

Glycine

Alanine

10.3 Proteins are amino acid polymers

To form a protein, amino acids are hooked to each other through a particular type of bond. The bond between two amino acids is called a peptide (pep-tīd) bond. A peptide bond occurs only between the amine group on one amino acid and the carbonyl group on the other amino acid. The "R" group is not involved in the bond.

Each amino acid in a protein is called a peptide unit. When fewer than 50 amino acids are hooked together, the molecule is usually called a polypeptide (po-lē-pep'-tīd).

However, when more than around 50 amino acids are connected, the molecule is called a protein.

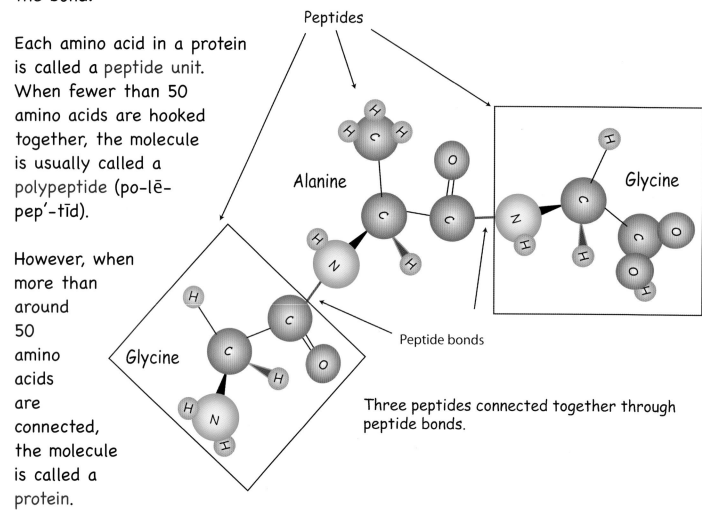

Peptides

Alanine

Glycine

Glycine

Peptide bonds

Three peptides connected together through peptide bonds.

10.4 Protein polymers form special shapes

Proteins don't remain stretched out chains. They fold into different shapes. Because protein molecules are made with many different amino acids, they have many different shapes. Some form coils, others fold into balls, and some combine with other proteins to form even more complicated shapes.

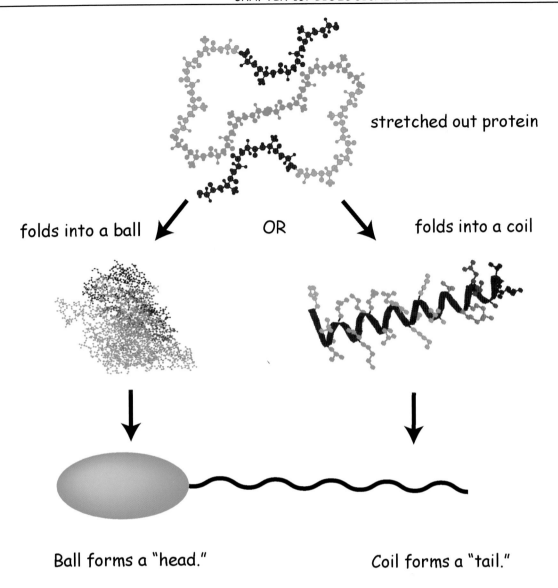

stretched out protein

folds into a ball   OR   folds into a coil

Ball forms a "head."   Coil forms a "tail."

Kinesin head and tail

For example, the protein kinesin (ki-nē'-sin) has a head shaped like a ball and a tail made out of a long coil. Why are shapes important? Because...

...the shape (structure) of a protein controls what it does

Kinesin "walks" along a molecular "road" inside our cells. Kinesin is a protein that moves things around inside your cells. It acts like a little delivery truck that carries new parts from the places where they are made to the places they are needed in the cell. A full kinesin has two heads (that work like feet) and two tails wound together. It moves along a molecular road called a microtubule (mī-krō-tü'-byül) to deliver the cargo.

Kinesin "walks" along a molecular "road" and carries cargo

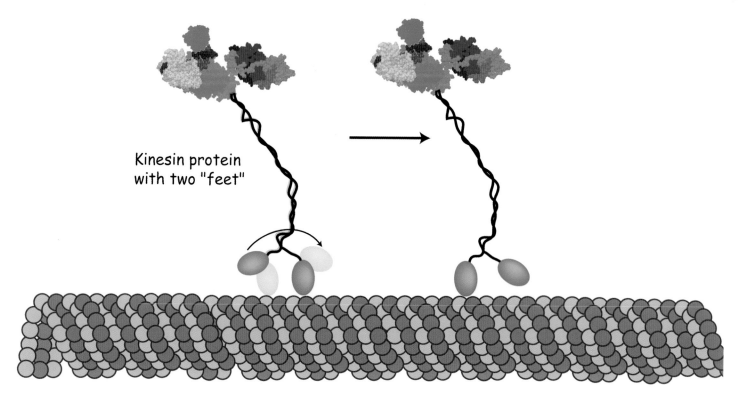

Kinesin protein
with two "feet"

Molecular "road" (microtubule)

10.5 Protein machines

Because they can fold into many different shapes, proteins are like tiny *machines*. They can do an amazing number of things. For example, some proteins move molecules by "walking" like kinesin. Some are "pumps," some "read," some "cut," some "repair cuts," and others "build" or "assemble." These tiny machines do all of the work inside a cell!

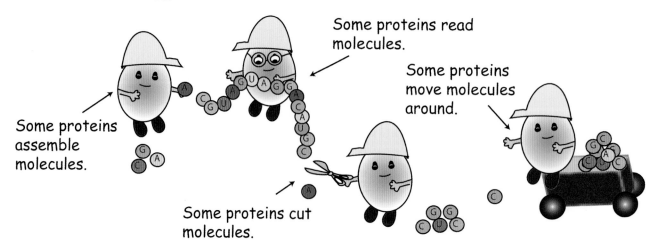

Some proteins read
molecules.

Some proteins
move molecules
around.

Some proteins
assemble
molecules.

Some proteins cut
molecules.

Proteins do all the work!

Kinesin is one such protein machine. Another is amylase (a'-mi-lās). Recall that in Chapter 8 we learned about starches, which are long chains of sugar molecules. Amylase is a "cutting" machine that cuts amylose, a starch, to get back the individual sugar molecules contained in it. Our bodies can then use these sugar molecules for energy.

We digest most of our food in our stomachs, but amylase is actually found in our mouth. It is in our saliva. When we eat food, the amylase begins to digest, or break down, amylose molecules in our mouth before we even swallow.

Sugar molecules

Amylase protein
(an amylose cutting machine)

Amylose

Amylase is a protein that breaks down amylose molecules into individual sugar molecules.

10.6 DNA

One of the molecules that proteins "read" and "cut" is DNA. DNA is an abbreviation that stands for deoxyribonucleic (dē-äk'-sē-rī'-bō-nü-klē'-ik) acid. Deoxyribonucleic acid (DNA) is a polymer that is made of *nucleotides*, which are made of two parts: bases and ribose sugars. The bases are connected to the sugars, and the sugars are connected to each other.

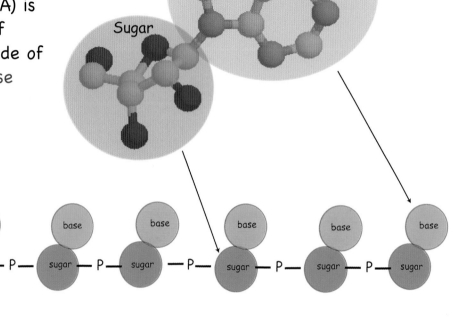

Base

Sugar

base — sugar — P — sugar — P — sugar — P — sugar — P — sugar — P — sugar
base   base   base   base   base   base

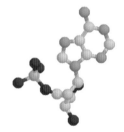

Adenosine monophosphate (AMP)

A

Guanosine monophosphate (GMP)

G

There are four bases that are used for the DNA polymer. They are called adenine (a'-də-nēn), guanine (gwä'-nēn), cytosine (sī'-tō-sēn), and thymine (thī'-mēn). They are given the single symbols A, G, C, and T.

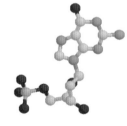

Cytosine monophosphate (CMP)

C

Thymidine monophosphate (TMP)

T

10.7 DNA structure

DNA is a very unique polymer. It is actually two strands of polymers wrapped around each other like a twisted ladder. The bases in the middle of the ladder interact with each other, and the ribose sugars form the sides of the ladder. This twisted shape is called a double helix.

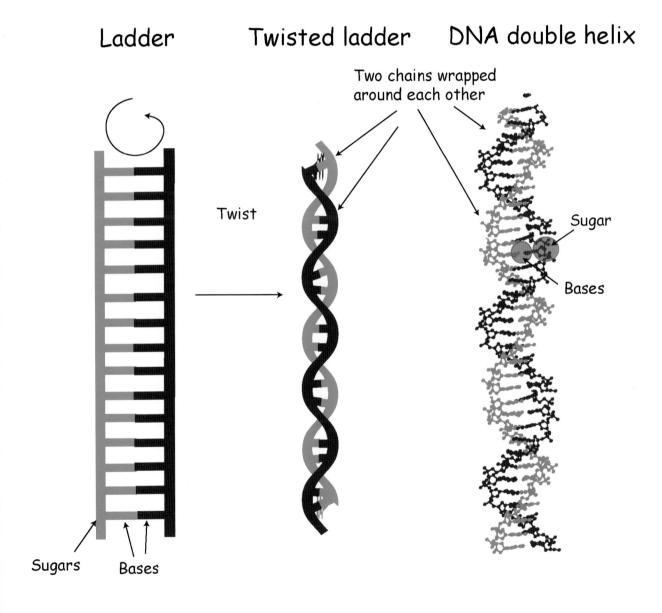

The bases (letters A, G, C, and T) along the DNA make up the genetic code. The letters of DNA can be read by protein "reading machines," just like we read a book. DNA is the "library" for our cells, and the letters store all of the information cells need to run and make new cells.

10.8 Protein machines on DNA

DNA polymerase (pō-li′-mər-ās) is a "DNA copy machine" that makes new copies of the DNA library. It is called a polymerase because it makes a DNA polymer. The polymerase "holds" the DNA, much as one might hold a rope. It crawls along the DNA, adding new nucleotides as it goes.

DNA polymerase on DNA

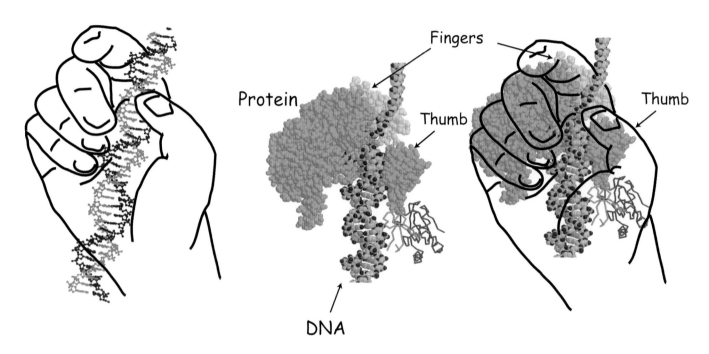

There are many kinds of polymerases that assemble other types of nucleic acid polymers, but all have the same basic structure because they all need to accomplish the same task. Again, the structure of a protein is partly determined by the task it needs to perform.

10.9 Summary

Here are the most important points to remember from this chapter:

º Proteins and DNA are polymers inside our bodies.

º Proteins do all of the work inside cells including moving molecules, making molecules, and cutting and assembling molecules.

º DNA carries the genetic code, which tells cells how to grow.

Glossary-Index

Acid-base indicator ◦ a dye that changes color when pH changes, 23, 24.

Acid-base reaction ◦ a particular type of chemical reaction in which an acid neutralizes a base, 21.

Adenine (a'-də-nēn) [A] ◦ one of the four nucleic acid bases that make DNA, 62.

Alkali (al'-kə-lī) metals ◦ the group of elements in the far left-hand column of the periodic table, 6.

Alkaline (al'-kə-līn) metals ◦ the group of elements in the column just to the right of the alkali metals, 6.

Amine (ə'-mēn) group ◦ [-NH$_2$] two hydrogen atoms connected to a nitrogen atom which is connected to another molecule, 57.

Amino (ə-mē'-nō) acid ◦ a molecule with a central carbon atom that has a carboxylic acid group, an amine group, and an "R" group attached, 57.

Amylase (a'-mi-lās) ◦ the protein that breaks down amylose into individual glucose molecules, 61.

Amylose (a'-mi-lōs) ◦ a common unbranched polysaccharide found in plants, 48.

Amylopectin (a-mi-lō-pek'-tin) ◦ a common branched polysaccharide found in plants, 48.

Atomic number ◦ the number located in the upper left-hand corner near the atomic symbol. It tells the number of protons in an atom's nucleus, 4.

Atomic weight ◦ the combined weight of an atom's protons and neutrons, 5.

Atoms (a-təms) ◦ [atomos, Gr.] a fundamental unit of all matter composed of protons, neutrons, and electrons, 2.

Axis (pl. axes) ◦ the main vertical or horizontal line on a plot, 29.

Bond ◦ the attachment between two atoms in a molecule. A chemical bond can be either covalent or ionic, 9.

Carbohydrate (kär-bō-hī'-drāt) ◦ [carbo –carbon, hydrate-water] any of a variety of compounds that are made of carbon and water, 46, 47.

Carbon ◦ the sixth element on the periodic table with 6 protons, 6 neutrons, and 6 electrons. It has the symbol C, 4.

Carboxylic (kär-bäk-si'-lic) acid group ◦ [-COOH] a carbon, hydrogen, and two oxygen atoms, 57.

Cellulose (sel'-yoo-lōs) ◦ the polysaccharide that is the main structural molecule in plants, 48, 49.

Chemistry ◦ the field of science that studies the composition, structure and properties of matter, 2.

Chemical elements ◦ all of the atoms that make up living and non-living things, 4.

Chromatography (krō-mə-tä'-grə-fē) ◦ [chroma, Gr. color; graphe, Gr. to write] a method for separating mixtures by passing a solution over a solid film or powder, 43.

Citric (si'-trik) acid ◦ an acid found in various fruits including grapefruit and oranges, 22.

Chemical reaction ◦ occurs when bonds between atoms and molecules are created or destroyed, 15.

Combination (käm-bə-nā-shən) reaction ◦ when two or more molecules combine with each other to make a new molecule, 15.

Concentration (kän-sen-trā'-shən) ◦ the number of molecules in a given volume of solution, 27

Covalent (cō-vā'-lent) bond ◦ attachment formed when two atoms are joined together and share their electrons, 10.

Cross-links ◦ the links between two polymer molecules (long chains of molecules), 54.

Cytosine (sī'-tō-sēn) [C] ◦ one of the four nucleic acid bases that make DNA, 62.

Decomposition (dē-käm-pō-zi'-shən) reaction ◦ occurs when a molecule breaks apart into two or more molecules, 15, 16.

Deoxyribonucleic acid (dē-äk'-sē-rī'-bō-nü-klē'-ik) [DNA] ◦ a polymer of A, T, G, and C that carries the genetic code, 62.

Dilute (dī-loot') ◦ a solution with few molecules per unit volume, 27.

Displacement (dis-plās'-mənt) reaction ◦ occurs when one atom displaces another atom during a chemical reaction, 15, 16.

Dissolve ◦ occurs when a liquid like water causes the molecules in a solid to break apart from each other and become loose in solution, 35.

Double helix ◦ the structure formed by two strands of DNA wrapped around each other, 63.

DNA (see deoxyribonucleic acid).

DNA polymerase (pō-li'-mər-ās) ◦ the protein that copies DNA inside a cell, 64.

Spontaneous (spän-tā'-nē-əs) ○ occurs when a chemical reaction proceeds without added energy input, 17.

Starch ○ polysaccharides that are found in both plants and animals, 48.

Symbol ○ a unique symbol given to each chemical element. It is usually the first two letters of the element name, 4.

Table salt (see sodium chloride)

Thymine (thī'-mēn) [T] ○ one of the four nucleic acid bases that make DNA, 62.

Titration (tī-trā'-shən) ○ the experimental technique used to find out the unknown concentration of an acid or base, 28, 30.

Tungsten ○ [Wolfram, German] element number 74 with the chemical symbol W. Tungsten has 74 protons, 74 electrons, and 109 neutrons, 4.

Uranium (yü-rā'-nē-əm) ○ element number 92 with the chemical symbol U. Uranium has 92 protons, 92 electrons, and 146 neutrons, 5.

Vegetable oil ○ [glycerol trioleate], 37.

Vinegar ○ a dilute solution of acetic acid, 26, 27.

Vulcanization (vul-kə-nī-zā'-shən) ○ the process changing the properties of sticky natural rubber into a more usable form with the use of high heat and sulfur, 54.

Water ○ [H_2O] the molecule formed by two hydrogen atoms and one oxygen atom, 12.

Pronunciation Key

a	add	k	cool	u	up
ā	race	l	love	ü	sue
ä	palm	m	move	v	vase
â(r)	air	n	nice	w	way
b	bat	ng	sing	y	yarn
ch	check	o	odd	z	zebra
d	dog	ō	open		
e	end	ô	jaw	ə	a in above
ē	tree	oi	oil		e in sicken
f	fit	oo	pool		i in possible
g	go	p	pit		o in melon
h	hope	r	run		u in circus
i	it	s	sea		
ī	ice	sh	sure		
j	joy	t	take		